The Ever Fresh Words Of The Heart

Matt Theo Coles

BookLeaf Publishing
India | USA | UK

Copyright © Matt Theo Coles
All Rights Reserved.

This book has been self-published with all reasonable efforts taken to make the material error-free by the author. No part of this book shall be used, reproduced in any manner whatsoever without written permission from the author, except in the case of brief quotations embodied in critical articles and reviews.

The Author of this book is solely responsible and liable for its content including but not limited to the views, representations, descriptions, statements, information, opinions, and references ["Content"]. The Content of this book shall not constitute or be construed or deemed to reflect the opinion or expression of the Publisher or Editor. Neither the Publisher nor Editor endorse or approve the Content of this book or guarantee the reliability, accuracy, or completeness of the Content published herein and do not make any representations or warranties of any kind, express or implied, including but not limited to the implied warranties of merchantability, fitness for a particular purpose.

The Publisher and Editor shall not be liable whatsoever...

Made with ❤ on the BookLeaf Publishing Platform
www.bookleafpub.in
www.bookleafpub.com

Dedication

For those with wounds and those without. For those with hearts and souls unbound by the limits of the world. We search, we reach for the stars, we find interstellar avenues, and find ourselves.

Preface

This book is not just a collection of poems, it is a map to the soul. It is a series of thoughts I've had day after day and year after year. I originally thought I would publish a book based on my though-experiments, but when I was presented with the opportunity to write a poetry book, I found a beautiful marriage between my poetry and my thoughts-per-day experiment.

These words are born from my mind and from the quiet place beneath thought: the place where breath becomes prayer, where stillness becomes music, where the self remembers it is eternal.

These poems are invitations to experience life in different ways. They do not ask to be understood, but felt. They are mirrors, reflecting the truth that the Divine has planted within every human heart.

We live in a world that teaches us to seek validation, identity, and purpose from the outside, from people, possessions, achievements, and roles. But what you hold in your hands is a return to the inner world, the place where you are already whole, already connected, already guided.

You are not reading these poems.
You are remembering them.

Because the wisdom found here does not belong to the me, it belongs to every soul longing to awaken.

This book is for the one who senses there is more to life than what can be seen.
For the one who has tasted both suffering and joy and knows there is gold hidden in both.
For the one who wishes not merely to live, but to become.

May these words serve as a compass pointing you back to your own heartbeat,
your own breath,
your own sacred frequency.

The journey is as much inward as it is outward.

And as you step into these pages, know that
as you seek truth, truth seeks you.

Acknowledgements

For everyone I love

1. Your Tomorrow Self

Do not live only for this breath, beloved.
For already,
another version of you
waits at the horizon of dawn,
hands open
to receive what you plant today.

Greet the world with kindness,
even when the heart is weary
for the smile you offer a stranger now
will one day return
as a balm upon your own soul.

There are tasks you resist,
burdens you do not wish to lift
carry them anyway.
Each step you take in service of tomorrow
is a jewel placed lovingly
into your future palm.

Your tomorrow self
is not a stranger.
It is the child of this moment,

and you are its parent.
Feed it with discipline,
clothe it with compassion,
and it will one day rise
to thank you
with a radiant heart.

So act today
as if you are already
receiving the embrace
of your wiser, future self
for truly,
that embrace is God's.

2. Where Vibrations Sing

Your heart is the sacred drum
beating the rhythm of the unseen.
Let the mind fall silent.

Thoughts are like clouds
Dissipating over a radiant moon.

Send your frequency into the ether.
For the calm and the storm,
the stillness and the stirring,
are both within you.

Feel the oscillation,
this pure state of being
where sound becomes light
and light becomes prayer.

Continue
until every boundary dissolves,
until no difference remains
between your breath
and the breath of the universe
until you can no longer tell

where it begins
and where you end.

3. The Tune Of What Was Once You

You have already lived this life
to its final breath.
Your bones have returned to dust,
your name to silence.

Now, as a soul freed from the body,
you are invited to watch
what once was called you.

See how you drive across the earth,
how your hands prepare food,
how you hold your children,
how you speak to your friends.

Watch how you treat
the one who shares your heart
every word a ripple
in the ocean of eternity.

You are both the memory
and the moment.
The ghost and the living flame.
The one who has died,

and the one still choosing
how to live.

From this sacred distance
you remember:
This is what you were like.

And from the beating center
of this moment
you realize:
This is what you are becoming.

This life
is not a line you travel
it is a mirror
in which the eternal
recognizes itself.

4. Allow Love To Permeate The Present

Sweat every day
let your body become
a temple of gratitude,
each drop
a silent Amen.

Laugh
as if every prayer
has already been answered,
for laughter is the sound
of God rising in your chest.

And love,
love
as if it is the only language
the universe has ever spoken.

Because it is.
Before words were born,
before stars took form,
love was the first vibration
and all of creation

is still echoing
its song.

5. Do Not Be Distracted By The Nonvisceral

Recognize yourself within your body
not as a prisoner,
but as a king seated on a living throne.

These hands are not strangers.
They are servants of the soul.
What work are they doing?
Are they washing dishes
in the rhythm of devotion?
Or are they lost in endless scrolling,
forgetting their noble purpose?

Look gently at your thumb,
moving upward again and again
a monk repeating
a prayer of distraction.
How many moments
has this motion stolen
from your destiny?

Be mindful of this body
how you sit,
how you walk,

how you breathe.
This vessel is magnificent,
capable of miracles
when guided by presence.

Do not abandon it to habit.
Reclaim it
with reverence.
For your body is not just flesh
it is a doorway
through which the Divine
enters the world.

6. Glory Be To God

For this season of the soul,
I choose to want nothing.

Not the new,
not the old.
Not beauty,
not its absence.
I let things be
as God has made them
neither clinging nor rejecting,
only witnessing.

If I make myself beautiful,
it is not from vanity,
but reverence
the way a priest
sets flowers on the altar.

If I am kind, let it be
not from desire to be good,
but because kindness
is the natural fragrance
of the soul.
And if I fail,

let that too be held gently,
for I do not seek the praise
of even my own heart.

I do not ask the car to run
or to break.
If it moves,
I whisper "Glory be to God."
If it stops,
I whisper the same.

For there is only one longing left in me:
not for comfort or perfection,
but for Grace
Grace that falls like rain
on all that I am
and all that I am not.

Beloved,
take every want from me
until only You remain.

7. Take It Day By Day

Day One
Breathe.
Let every inhale remind you:
You are alive by God's permission.
Let every exhale be a surrender.

Day Two
Breathe again, as if for the first time
until breath is no longer yours,
but the Beloved breathing you.

Day Three
Now slow the river.
Straighten the spine
become a candle,
its flame unmoving yet alive.

Day Four
Open the gates of perception.
Quiet thought,
and watch how creation pours in
each leaf a revelation,
each bird a messenger of God.

Day Five

Receive it again, with deeper eyes.
This world is not scenery—
it is scripture written
in mountains, rivers, and wind.

Day Six

Speak the truth to another soul.
Open your heart
as you would open your hands in prayer.
Let honesty become the bridge
between two spirits longing to be seen.

Day Seven

Now speak truth to yourself.
Remove every veil,
bow before your own soul.
In that nakedness
you will find the face of God
smiling through you.

8. In This Electric Body

You are alive!
Do not sleep through this miracle.

Feel the earth beneath your bare feet
it has been waiting a thousand years
just to touch you.

Let the warm water of the shower
roll over your skin
like bathing in Gods oceans.

Feel the cool air
kiss your damp body
a silent hymn of awakening.

Taste your food as if it were
the first fruit in Eden.
Let each bite be a verse of praise
sung inside your soul.

Hug your children
and feel the universe
rushing back into your heart
as love returning home.

Hug your parents
and know you are holding
the roots from which
your very being blossomed.

To be alive
is the greatest worship.
Do not forget
this moment
is God,
experiencing Life
through you.
You are alive

9. Let The Light Shine Through

Everything that breaks
is an invitation
to reveal your hidden beauty.

Mend the shattered
with gold
not to hide the cracks,
but to honor them.
For what once was broken
now carries the story
of its resurrection.

Every wound, every sorrow,
every moment of shame
is not a flaw to conceal,
but a doorway
through which the Light enters.

Do not discard what is damaged.
Do not numb your pain
with distraction and denial.
Sit with it.
Fill it with awareness,

with love.
This is how the soul becomes art.

In this world of things
own only what you are willing to care for.
If it breaks,
mend it with reverence.
For what you restore
becomes more sacred
than what was never touched
by suffering.

Let your life become
a vessel of golden seams
each crack a testament
to the Beauty of Becoming.

10. The Darkness

I have walked through valleys
where regret clung to me like night
I have seen the shadows of my past
reach out to pull me back.

God whispers:
Do not build your home in sorrow.
Keep moving, keep moving.
For every step toward the Light
erases a thousand steps in darkness.

Guilt is a chain
for those who forget
that God is always waiting
with open arms.

So I forgive myself,
and lay lanterns of love
along the path ahead.
Let others forgive me too
but if they do not,
still I walk toward dawn.

Right now

is the only holy moment.
Begin here.
Plant your foot in light,
lift the next step in love.

There is no room in this heart
for guilt to live
only space for transformation.
Only room for the Beloved
to write the rest
of the story.

11. Even The Brightest Stars Burn Out

Once I fastened my heart
to people,
to cities,
to my own name
forgetting that every form
is a traveler
who must one day depart.

All that I clung to
was water in my hands.
The skyline drifted like a cloud,
names faded like incense in the wind.
Permanence was only a story
my longing told me.

Then the Beloved whispered:

Do not tie your soul
to what is passing.
Tie it to the fire I placed within you
before you were born.

Attach yourself to purpose,

for purpose is My hand
guiding you through the waves.
Not a person, job, or place
those are rivers
that change their course.

Your mission is the anchor.
When the current pulls you in again,
drop into the depths of the heart
and sink into the Timeless.

Even the brightest stars burn out,
and lovers drift into other skies.
But meaning hums beneath all things
a pulse,
a hidden heartbeat of God.

It is not the hands that keep you safe,
but the reaching toward Me.
Not the home that makes you whole,
but the road that teaches you
your real name.

So attach yourself to purpose
not because you need it,
but because it is already you.

And know this secret:
that Purpose is Love,
and Love
is the Beloved
calling you home.

12. Suffer The Truth

You will suffer in this world
this is the way of clay
shaped by the Divine Hand.
But listen closely:
you may suffer as gold in the furnace,
or as dust swept by the wind.

You either suffer
for what your soul truly longs for,
or you suffer
from what your ego clings to.
Both paths have pain
but only one
leads you back to God.

The world keeps moving
like a caravan in the night.
You may chase after its shadows,
bruising your heart on illusions,
or bleed for something real
a purpose lit by God's breath.

Suffer the work
and reap the light,

or suffer the emptiness
that howls in every unchosen moment.
The pain will come regardless
but you, beloved,
you are free to choose
what it is made of.

Every dream asks its price.
Every step toward truth
costs a part of the false self.
Growth or decay
there is no stillness here.
Every breath moves you
toward union or separation.

So choose your suffering wisely.
Let it be the kind
that polishes your soul
and draws you into the arms of the Eternal.

For in the end,
the only mercy in this life
is to suffer for Love
and find that Love,
at last,
has suffered every step
with you.

13. The Sweet And The Bitter

No one is coming for you,
because you were never alone.
The ether is not empty,
it is filled with light.

The good and the bad
are simply waves
returning you to the ocean of yourself.

Why wait for footsteps at the door
when the One you seek
is already knocking
from within your heart?

Taste this moment
its sweetness, its sharpness
all of it is nourishment
for the soul is awakening.

The stars are not far away;
they rise inside your chest.

14. A Rising Soul

You are a mosaic of stardust,
carried gently through generations
in the hidden vaults of bone.
Every heartbeat is a secret poem
the Beloved is reciting through you.

The music within your soul
waits not for the world's ear,
but for your own awakening.
Turn the key,
and the universe will sing your name.

Find the act that builds you,
and your spirit will rise like dawn.
It may be a single breath of courage,
or a leap into the light of many eyes.
You are the only one of your kind
a note that has never been played before.
Confidence is not pride
it is the compass of the soul
pointing you back to God.

If you do not yet know your path,
wander in wonder,

taste the edge of your fear.
To live fully is a kind of worship;
to die into truth is a kind of birth.

Each step into the unknown
is your soul whispering,
"This is why you came."

Your wings were never broken
only folded in stillness.
Lift your gaze toward the Infinite,
and they will remember their flight.

So seek what builds you.
Let your inner light step forward.
You are a living mosaic of Love's design,
and there is holy magic in your being.

Confidence is the call of the Beloved
answer it,
and be renewed.
For the world is quietly waiting
for the unveiling
of the one and only
you.

15. At Peace

Be patient, dear heart,
for the river knows its way to the sea.

Be at peace,
for every breath was written
before the first star was born.

Lay down your unsettled thoughs.
The mind is a lantern,
but God is the sunrise.

What is yours will arrive
without error, without hurry.

Trust the One
who spins galaxies from silence
you are already held
in His hands.

16. Unique As A Flame

Your perspective is a lamp
lit by the hand of God.
Guard it well,
for no other light
was placed in your soul
exactly as this one.

When you meet another's flame,
do not be afraid
you may borrow its warmth,
you may let it teach you how to shine
but never trade your lamp
for one that was not
born in your heart.

The sorrow of this age
comes from forgetting
the holy fire within,
trading the voice of the Beloved
for echoes in empty halls.

Return to your own seeing.
Cherish it.
Nurture it.

For through your eyes,
the Divine
is looking at the world.

17. Unmoved By The Noise

Speak slowly,
as one who has just returned from the ocean of silence.
Let your voice carry the depth
of one who knows eternity is listening.

And when a small noise rises against you
a complaint, an insult,
a restless ego squeaking like a wheel in need of oil
do not be disturbed.

That sound is only a spark
falling into the vast night.
You are not the spark.
You are the night.

Do not be offended.
Offense is for those
who believe themselves separate.
Instead, smile inwardly and remember:
in this universe of whirling galaxies,
a single voice of anger
is no more than an ant shouting at a mountain.

Be the mountain.

Be the stillness.
Let every squeak remind you
of the greatness of your own eternity

18. Planted In The Present

There is no great mountain of worry
pressing upon your soul.
There is only the next breath,
the next step,
the next grain of rice
placed gently in the bowl of this moment.

Life is not a maze
built to confuse you.
It is a single path
opening beneath your feet
as you walk it.

Only the mind, drunk on shadows,
tries to turn a candle flame
into a forest fire.

Be simple as the dawn
take what is before you
and give it your full heart.

The whole universe exists
only in this present moment.

Whoever lives here
is free.

19. The Silence Is The Music

Everything in this world is singing.
Not with words,
but with the secret pulse of being.

You are a flute
through which the breath of the Divine
is always flowing.
Listen
what song is moving through you?
Is it fear trembling in the reed,
or love turning each note to light?

What you project,
the world receives.
Every heart that meets you
is tuning itself
to your hidden melody.

So become peace,
and peace will echo back to you.
Become love,
and love will rise to meet you
like dawn meeting the horizon.